GW01607130

PRAYERS

of a

Righteous MAN

PRAYERS

of a

Righteous MAN

THIRD EDITION

Brighton Books
Nashville, TN 37203

The quoted ideas expressed in this book (but not Scripture verses) are not, in all cases, exact quotations, as some have been edited for clarity and brevity. In all cases, the author has attempted to maintain the speaker's original intent. In some cases, quoted material for this book was obtained from secondary sources, primarily print media. While every effort was made to ensure the accuracy of these sources, the accuracy cannot be guaranteed. For additions, deletions, corrections, or clarifications in future editions of this text, please write Brighton Books.

Cover design & page layout by: Bart Dawson
Copy written and compiled by: Criswell Freeman

ISBN 1-58334-211-7

1 2 3 4 5 6 7 8 9 10 • 03 04 05 06 07 08 09 10

Printed in the United States of America

CONTENTS

The familiar saying is both tried and true: "How you start is how you finish." And so it is with the days of our lives.

When we begin each day with a few moments of quiet meditation and worship, we reap a multitude of blessings throughout the day. When we start our mornings with a time of devotional readings and prayer, we gain perspective and strength for the challenges ahead.

This book is intended to assist you in your daily devotional readings. As such, this text is divided into 31 chapters, one for each day of the month. Each chapter contains Bible verses, a brief essay, inspirational quotations from noted Christian thinkers, and a prayer.

During the next 31 days, please try this experiment: read a chapter each day. If you're already committed to a daily time of worship, this book will enrich that experience. If you are not, the simple act of giving God a few minutes each morning will change the direction and the quality of your life.

Every day provides opportunities to put God where He belongs: at the center of our lives. When we do so, we worship Him, not just with words but with deeds. And, we become dutiful servants of God, righteous men who share His Son's love and salvation with the world. May you be that righteous man.

Day 1

A Prayer for . . .

A RIGHTEOUS HEART

The righteous man walks in his integrity;
His children are blessed after him.

Proverbs 20:7 NKJV

God gave us His commandments for a reason: so that we might obey them and be blessed. Oswald Chambers, the author of the Christian classic devotional text *My Utmost for His Highest*, advised, "Never support an experience which does not have God as its source, and faith in God as its result." These words serve as a powerful reminder that, as Christians, we are called to walk with God and obey His commandments. But, we live in a world that presents us with countless temptations to stray far from God's path. When confronted with sin, we have clear instructions: Walk—or better yet run—in the opposite direction.

The Bible contains thorough instructions which, if followed, lead to fulfillment, righteousness, and salvation. But, if we choose to ignore God's commandments, the results are as predictable as they are tragic.

A righteous life has many components: faith, honesty, love, kindness, humility, gratitude, and worship, to name but a few. If we seek to follow the steps of our Savior, we must seek to live according to His commandments. Let us follow them, and let us conduct our lives in such a way that we might be shining examples for those who have not yet found Christ.

Bible history is filled with people who began the race with great success but failed at the end because they disregarded God's rules.

Warren Wiersbe

Nobody is good by accident.
No man ever became holy by chance.

C. H. Spurgeon

It may be said without qualification that every man is as holy and as full of the Spirit as he wants to be. He may not be as full as he wishes he were, but he is most certainly as full as he wants to be.

A. W. Tozer

Whoever pursues godliness and unfailing love will find life, godliness, and honor.

Proverbs 21:21 NLT

Dear Lord, this world is filled with so many temptations, distractions, and frustrations. When I turn my thoughts away from You and Your Word, I suffer. But when I turn my thoughts, my faith, and my prayers to You, I am safe. Direct my path, Father, and let me discover Your will for me today and every day that I live.

—

Amen

My Prayer for Today

Day 2

A Prayer for . . .

GOD'S GRACE

For all have sinned and fall short
of the glory of God, and are justified freely
by his grace through the redemption
that came by Christ Jesus.

Romans 3:23-24 NIV

Romans 3:23 reminds us that "all have sinned and fallen short of the glory of God." Despite our shortcomings, God sent His Son so that we might be redeemed from our sins. In doing so, our Heavenly Father demonstrated His infinite mercy and His infinite love.

We have received countless gifts from God, but none can compare with the gift of salvation. God's grace is the ultimate gift, and we owe Him the ultimate in thanksgiving. Let us praise the Creator for His priceless gift, and let us share the Good News with our families, with our friends, and with the world.

Christ sacrificed His life on the cross so that we might have eternal life. This gift, freely given from God's only begotten Son, is the priceless possession of everyone who accepts Him as Lord and Savior. We return our Savior's love by welcoming Him into our hearts and sharing His message and His love. When we do so, we are blessed here on earth *and* throughout all eternity.

The grace of God is sufficient for all our needs,
for every problem, and for every difficulty,
for every broken heart, and
for every human sorrow.

Peter Marshall

Number one, God brought me here. It is by His will that I am in this place. In that fact I will rest. Number two, He will keep me here in His love and give me grace to behave as His child. Number three, He will make the trial a blessing, teaching me the lessons He intends for me to learn and working in me the grace He means to bestow. Number four, in His good time He can bring me out again. How and when, He knows. So, let me say I am here.

Andrew Murray

This is love: not that we loved God,
but that he loved us and sent his Son
as an atoning sacrifice for our sins.

1 John 4:10 NIV

A Prayer for Today

Dear Lord, You have given Your grace freely through Christ Jesus. I praise You for that priceless gift. Let me share the Good News of Your Son with a world that desperately needs His peace, His abundance, His love, and His salvation.

—

Amen

My Prayer for Today

Day 3

A Prayer for . . .

A THANKFUL HEART

Give thanks in all circumstances; for this is God's will for you in Christ Jesus.

1 Thessalonians 5:18 NIV

The words of 1 Thessalonians 5:18 remind us to give thanks in every circumstance of life. But sometimes, when our hearts are troubled and our lives seem to be spinning out of control, we don't feel much like celebrating. Yet God's Word is clear: In all circumstances, our Father offers us His love, His strength, and His grace. And, in all circumstances, we must thank Him.

Have you thanked God today for blessings that are too numerous to count? Have you offered Him your heartfelt prayers and your wholehearted praise? If not, it's time to slow down and offer a prayer of thanksgiving to the One who has given you life on earth *and* life eternal.

If you are a thoughtful Christian, you will be a thankful Christian. No matter your circumstances, you owe God so much more than you can ever repay, and you owe Him your heartfelt thanks. So thank Him . . . and keep thanking Him, today, tomorrow, and forever.

Praise and thank God for who He is
and for what He has done for you.

Billy Graham

God is worthy of our praise and is pleased
when we come before Him with thanksgiving.

Shirley Dobson

It is only with gratitude that life becomes rich.

Dietrich Bonhoeffer

And let the peace of the Messiah,
to which you were also called in one body,
control your hearts. Be thankful.

Colossians 3:15 HCSB

A Prayer for Today

Dear Lord, sometimes, amid the demands of the day, I lose perspective, and I fail to give thanks for Your blessings and for Your love. Today, help me to count those blessings, and let me give thanks to You, Father, for Your love, for Your grace, for Your blessings, and for Your Son.

—

Amen

My Prayer for Today

Day 4

A Prayer for . . .

COURAGE

The LORD is my light and my salvation; whom shall I fear? The LORD is the strength of my life; of whom shall I be afraid?

Psalm 27:1 KJV

It has been said, quite correctly, that courage is not the absence of fear but the willingness to move ahead *in spite of* fear. All of us face fears, worries, and disappointments, but as believers we may be comforted in the certain knowledge that God is bigger than *all* our fears.

This world can be a dangerous and daunting place, but as Christians we have every reason to live courageously. After all, the ultimate battle has already been fought and won on the cross at Calvary. And, as Hannah Whitall Smith correctly observed, "When once we are assured that God is good, then there can be nothing left to fear."

The next time you find your courage tested to the limit, face your fears and take them to God. When you do, He will give you strength, wisdom, and courage. And remember this: whatever your challenge, whatever your trouble, God can handle it. And will.

The Lord is glad to open the gate to every knocking soul. It opens very freely; its hinges are not rusted, no bolts secure it. Have faith and enter at this moment through holy courage. If you knock with a heavy heart, you shall yet sing with joy of spirit. Never be discouraged!

C. H. Spurgeon

Faith is stronger than fear.

John Maxwell

Jesus Christ can make the weakest man into a divine dreadnought, fearing nothing.

Oswald Chambers

Do not be afraid or discouraged. For the LORD your God is with you wherever you go.

Joshua 1:9 NLT

Lord, sometimes, this world is a fearful place.
Yet, You have promised me that You are
with me always. Today, Dear Father,
I will live courageously as I place my trust
in Your everlasting power and my faith
in Your everlasting love.

—

Amen

My Prayer for Today

Day 5

A Prayer for . . .

FAITH

For truly I say to you, if you have faith as
a mustard seed, you shall say to this mountain,
"Move from here to there" and it shall move;
and nothing shall be impossible to you.

Matthew 17:20 NASB

Because we live in a demanding world, all of us have mountains to climb *and* mountains to move. Moving those mountains requires faith.

Are you a mountain mover whose faith is evident for all to see? Or, are you a spiritual shrinking violet? God needs more men who are willing to move mountains for His glory and for His kingdom.

Every life—including yours—is a series of successes and failures, celebrations and disappointments, joys and sorrows. Every step of the way, through every triumph and tragedy, God walks with you, ready and willing to strengthen you. Accept His strength today.

Jesus taught His disciples that if they had faith, they could move mountains. And you can too . . . *if* you have faith.

Let your faith in Christ be in the quiet confidence that He will, every day and every moment, keep you as the apple of His eye, keep you in perfect peace and in the sure experience of all the light and the strength you need.

Andrew Murray

I do not want merely to possess a faith; I want a faith that possesses me.

Charles Kingsley

Faith is to believe what you do not yet see; the reward for this faith is to see what you believe.

St. Augustine

Now faith is the reality of what is hoped for, the proof of what is not seen.

Hebrews 11:1 HCSB

A Prayer for Today

Dear Lord, make me Your obedient,
faithful servant. You are with me always.
Give me faith and let me remember that
with Your love and Your power,
I can live courageously and faithfully
today and every day.

—

Amen

My Prayer for Today

Day 6

A Prayer for . . .

PERSEVERANCE

For you need endurance, so that after you have
done God's will, you may receive
what was promised.

Hebrews 10:36 HCSB

In a world filled with roadblocks and stumbling blocks, we need strength, courage, and perseverance. And, as an example of perfect perseverance, we need look no further than our Savior, Jesus Christ.

Jesus finished what He began. Despite the torture He endured, despite the shame of the cross, Jesus was steadfast in His faithfulness to God. We, too, must remain faithful, especially during times of hardship.

Perhaps you are in a hurry for God to reveal His plans for your life. If so, be forewarned: God operates on His own timetable not yours. Sometimes, God may answer your prayers with silence, and when He does, you must patiently persevere. In times of trouble, you must remain steadfast and trust in the merciful goodness of your Heavenly Father. Whatever your problem, He can handle it. Your job is to keep persevering until He does.

Every achievement worth remembering is stained with the blood of diligence and scarred by the wounds of disappointment.

Charles Swindoll

You cannot persevere unless there is a trial in your life. There can be no victories without battles; there can be no peaks without valleys. If you want the blessing, you must be prepared to carry the burden and fight the battle. God has to balance privileges with responsibilities, blessings with burdens, or else you and I will become spoiled, pampered children.

Warren Wiersbe

Blessed is the man who perseveres under trial, because when he has stood the test, he will receive the crown of life that God has promised to those who love him.

James 1:12 NIV

Dear Lord, You are my God, and I can draw strength from You. Let me trust You, Father, in good times and in bad times. Let me persevere—even if my soul is troubled—and let me follow Your Son Jesus Christ this day and forever.

—

Amen

My Prayer for Today

Day 7

A Prayer for . . .

DISCIPLINE

For God did not give us a spirit of timidity,
but a spirit of power, of love
and of self-discipline.

2 Timothy 1:7 NIV

God's Word is clear: as believers, we are called to lead lives of discipline, diligence, moderation, and maturity. But the world often tempts us to behave otherwise. Everywhere we turn, or so it seems, we are faced with powerful temptations to behave in undisciplined, ungodly ways.

We live in a world in which leisure is glorified and misbehavior is glamorized. But God has other plans. He did not create us for lives of mischief or mediocrity; He created us for far greater things.

Life's greatest rewards seldom fall into our laps; to the contrary, God rewards diligence and righteousness just as certainly as He punishes laziness and sin. As believers in a just God, we should behave accordingly.

If one examines the secret behind
a championship football team, a magnificent
orchestra, or a successful business,
the principal ingredient is invariably discipline.

James Dobson

The alternative to discipline is disaster.

Vance Havner

Apply your heart to discipline
And your ears to words of knowledge.

Proverbs 23:12 NASB

A Prayer for Today

Heavenly Father, make me a man of discipline and righteousness. Let me teach others by the faithfulness of my conduct, and let me follow Your will and Your Word, today and every day.

—

Amen

My Prayer for Today

My Hopes & Prayers for Next Week

My Hopes & Prayers for Next Week

Day 8

A Prayer for . . .

SPEECH THAT IS PLEASING TO GOD

Let the words of my mouth, and the meditation of my heart, be acceptable in thy sight, O LORD, my strength and my redeemer.

Psalm 19:14 KJV

All too often, we underestimate the importance of the words we speak. Whether we realize it or not, our words carry great weight and great power. If our words are encouraging, we can lift others up; if our words are hurtful, we can hold others back.

The Bible reminds us that "reckless words pierce like a sword, but the tongue of the wise brings healing" (Proverbs 12:18 NIV). In other words, if we are to solve more problems than we start, we must measure our words carefully.

Do you seek to be a source of encouragement to others? And, do you seek to be a worthy ambassador for Christ? If so, you must speak words that are worthy of your Savior. So think before you speak. Avoid angry outbursts. Refrain from constant criticism. Terminate tantrums. Negate negativism. Cease from being cynical. Instead, use Christ as your guide, and speak words of encouragement and hope to a world that needs both.

When you talk, choose the very same words that you would use if Jesus were looking over your shoulder. Because He is.

Marie T. Freeman

The great test of a man's character is his tongue.

Oswald Chambers

Fill the heart with the love of Christ so that only truth and purity can come out of the mouth.

Warren Wiersbe

Reckless words pierce like a sword, but the tongue of the wise brings healing.

Proverbs 12:18 NIV

Dear Lord, You hear every word that I say. Let my speech bring honor to You and to Your Son. Today and every day, let me speak words that are honest, kind, sincere, and worthy of You.

—

Amen

My Prayer for Today

Day 9

A Prayer for . . .

OUR FAMILIES

Choose for yourselves this day whom
you will serve . . . as for me and my household,
we will serve the LORD.

Joshua 24:15 NIV

In a world filled with countless obligations and frequent frustrations, we may be tempted to take our families for granted. But God intends otherwise.

Our families are precious gifts from our Father in heaven. If we are to be the righteous men that God intends, we must care for our families, we must love our families, we must lead our families, and we must make time for our families, even when the demands of the day are great.

No family is perfect, and neither is yours. But, despite the inevitable challenges, obligations, and hurt feelings of family life, your clan is God's blessing to you. That little band of men, women, and children is a priceless treasure on temporary loan from the Father above. Give thanks to the Giver for the gift of family . . . and act accordingly.

Apart from religious influence, the family is the most important influence on society.

Billy Graham

A home is a place where we find direction.

Gigi Graham Tchividjian

We must strengthen our commitment to model strong families ourselves, to live by godly priorities in a culture where self so often supersedes commitment to others. And, as we not only model but assertively reach out to help others, we must realize that even huge societal problems are solved one person at a time.

Chuck Colson

Their first responsibility is to show godliness at home and repay their parents by taking care of them. This is something that pleases God very much.

1 Timothy 5:4 NLT

A Prayer for Today

Dear Lord, make me a worthy example to all and a godly example to my family. Give me the wisdom to obey Your commandments and the courage to follow Your will. Let me lead my family in the ways that You would have us go, and let my home be one where Christ is honored today and forever.

—

Amen

My Prayer for Today

Day 10

A Prayer for . . .

GOD'S ABUNDANCE

And in that day you will ask Me nothing.
Most assuredly, I say to you, whatever you ask
the Father in My name He will give you.
Until now you have asked nothing in My name.
Ask, and you will receive,
that your joy may be full.

John 16:23-24 NKJV

The Word of God is clear: Christ came in order that we might have life abundant and life eternal. Eternal life is the priceless possession of *all* who invite Christ into their hearts, but God's abundance is optional: He *does not* force it upon us.

When we entrust our hearts and our days to the One who created us, we experience abundance through the grace and sacrifice of His Son. But, when we turn our thoughts and direct our energies away from God's commandments, we inevitably forfeit the spiritual abundance that might otherwise be ours.

Do you sincerely seek the riches that our Savior offers to those who give themselves to Him? Then follow Him completely and obey Him without reservation. When you do, you will receive the love and the abundance that He has promised. Seek first the salvation available through a personal relationship with Jesus Christ, and then claim the joy, the peace, and the spiritual abundance that the Shepherd offers His sheep.

God is the giver, and we are the receivers. And His richest gifts are bestowed not upon those who do the greatest things, but upon those who accept His abundance and His grace.

Hannah Whitall Smith

The Lord has abundantly blessed me all of my life. I'm not trying to pay Him back for all of His wonderful gifts; I just realize that He gave them to me to give away.

Lisa Whelchel

I will make you a great nation and I will bless you; I will make your name great, and you will be a blessing.

Genesis 12:2 NIV

Every good and perfect gift is from above, coming down from the Father of the heavenly lights . . . .

James 1:17 NIV

Thank You, Father, for the abundant life that is mine through Christ Jesus. Guide me according to Your will, and help me to be a worthy servant through all that I say and do. Give me courage, Lord, to claim the rewards You have promised, and when I do, let all the glory be Yours.

—

Amen

My Prayer for Today

Day 11

A Prayer for . . .

FRIENDSHIPS THAT ARE PLEASING TO GOD

Blessed in the man who does not walk in
the counsel of the wicked or stand in the way
of sinners or sit in the seat of mockers. But his
delight is in the law of the LORD, and on his law
he meditates day and night. He is like a tree
planted by streams of water, which yields its
fruit in season and whose leaf does not wither.
Whatever he does prospers.

Psalm 1:1-3 NIV

If we seek to live righteous lives, we must select friends who will encourage us to live righteously. Some friendships help us honor God; these friendships should be nurtured. Other friendships place us in situations where we are tempted to dishonor God by disobeying His commandments; friendships that dishonor God have the potential to do us great harm.

Because we tend to become like our friends, we must choose our friends carefully. Because our friends influence us in ways that are both subtle and powerful, we must ensure that our friendships are pleasing to God. When we spend our days in the presence of godly believers, we are blessed, not only by those friends but also by our Creator.

Do you seek to live a life that is pleasing to God? If so, you should build friendships that are pleasing to Him. When you do, your Heavenly Father will bless you and your friends with gifts that are simply too numerous to count.

A friend is one who makes me do my best.
Oswald Chambers

Friendship is one of the sweetest joys of life. Many might have failed beneath the bitterness of their trial had they not found a faithful, godly friend.
C. H. Spurgeon

For better or worse, you will eventually become more and more like the people you associate with. So why not associate with people who make you better, not worse?
Marie T. Freeman

Do not be misled:
"Bad company corrupts good character."
1 Corinthians 15:33 NIV

A Prayer for Today

Dear Lord, let me be a faithful friend to others, and let me be an example of righteous behavior to my friends, to my family, and to the world. I thank You, Lord, for friends who challenge me to become a better man; let me do the same for them today and every day.

—

Amen

My Prayer for Today

Day 12

A Prayer for . . .

A SERVANT'S HEART

The greatest among you will be your servant.
Whoever exalts himself will be humbled,
and whoever humbles himself will be exalted.

Matthew 23:11-12 HCSB

How do you achieve greatness in the eyes of God? By making yourself a humble servant. Of course, being a fallible human being, you may feel the temptation to build yourself up in the eyes of your neighbors. Resist that temptation. Instead, serve your neighbors quietly and without fanfare. Find a need and fill it . . . humbly. Lend a helping hand and share a word of kindness . . . anonymously. Take the time to minister to those in need.

Then, when you have done your best to serve your neighbors and to serve your God, you can rest comfortably, knowing that in the eyes of your Heavenly Father you have achieved greatness. And God's eyes, after all, are the only ones that really count.

That's what I love about serving God.
In His eyes, there are no little people . . .
because there are no big people.
We are all on the same playing field.

Joni Eareckson Tada

In the great orchestra we call life, you have an instrument and a song, and you owe it to God to play them both sublimely.

Max Lucado

I can usually sense that a leading is from the Holy Spirit when it calls me to humble myself, serve somebody, encourage somebody or give something away. Very rarely will the evil one lead us to do those kinds of things.

Bill Hybels

Your attitude should be the same as that of Christ Jesus . . .Who . . . made himself nothing, taking the very nature of a servant . . . .

Philippians 2:5, 7 NIV

Dear Lord, give me a servant's heart. When Jesus humbled Himself and became a servant, He also became an example for His followers. Make me a faithful steward of my gifts, and let me share with those in need.

—

Amen

My Prayer for Today

Day 13

A Prayer for . . .

OBEDIENCE

Jesus answered and said to him, "If anyone loves Me, he will keep My word; and My Father will love him, and We will come to him and make Our home with him."

John 14:23 NKJV

Obedience to God is determined not by words but by deeds. Talking about righteousness is easy; living righteously is far more difficult, especially in today's temptation-filled world.

Since God created Adam and Eve, we human beings have been rebelling against our Creator. Why? Because we are unwilling to trust God's Word, and we are unwilling to follow His commandments. God has given us a guidebook for righteous living called the Holy Bible. It contains thorough instructions which, if followed, lead to fulfillment, righteousness, and salvation. But, if we choose to ignore God's commandments, the results are as predictable as they are tragic.

Unless we are willing to abide by God's laws, all of our righteous proclamations ring hollow. How can we best proclaim our love for the Lord? By obeying Him. And, for further instructions, read the manual.

Only he who believes is obedient.
Only he who is obedient believes.

Dietrich Bonhoeffer

Obedience is the outward expression
of your love of God.

Henry Blackaby

Obedience that is not motivated by love
cannot produce the spiritual fruit
that God wants from His children.

Warren Wiersbe

And he that keepeth his commandments
dwelleth in him, and he in him. And hereby
we know that he abideth in us,
by the Spirit which he hath given us.

1 John 3:24 KJV

Dear Lord, when I obey Your commandments, and when I trust the promises of Your Son, I experience love, peace, and abundance. Direct my path far from the temptations and distractions of this world. And, let me discover Your will and follow it, Dear Lord, this day and always.

—

Amen

My Prayer for Today

Day 14

A Prayer for . . .

THE POWER TO ENCOURAGE OTHERS

Encourage each other. Live in harmony and peace. Then the God of love and peace will be with you.

2 Corinthians 13:11 NLT

Life is a team sport, and all of us need occasional pats on the back from our teammates. This world can be a difficult place, a place where many of our friends and family members are troubled by the challenges of everyday life. And since we cannot always be certain who needs our help, we should strive to speak helpful words to all those who cross our paths.

In the Book of Ephesians, Paul writes, "Do not let any unwholesome talk come out of your mouths, but only what is helpful for building others up according to their needs, that it may benefit those who listen" (4:29 NIV). Paul reminds us that when we choose our words carefully, we can have a powerful impact on those around us.

Today, let us be cheerful Christians; let us keep smiles on our faces and encouraging words on our lips. By blessing others, we also bless ourselves, and, at the same time, we do honor to the One who gave His life for us.

Make it a rule, and pray to God to help you to keep it, never to lie down at night without being able to say: "I have made at least one human being a little wiser, a little happier, or a little better this day."

Charles Kingsley

A lot of people have gone further than they thought they could because someone else thought they could.

Zig Ziglar

Encouragement is the oxygen of the soul.

John Maxwell

Let us consider how to stimulate one another to love and good deeds.

Hebrews 10:24 NASB

Dear Heavenly Father, because I am Your child,
I am blessed. You have lifted me up, Lord,
let me lift up others in a spirit of encouragement
and optimism and hope. And, if I can help
a fellow traveler, even in a small way,
Dear Lord, may the glory be Yours.

—

Amen

My Prayer for Today

My Hopes & Prayers for Next Week

My Hopes & Prayers for Next Week

Day 15

A Prayer for . . .

THE COURAGE TO SHARE THE GOOD NEWS

And I say to you, everyone who confesses
Me before men, the Son of Man will confess him
also before the angels of God . . . .

Luke 12:8 NASB

The Good News of our Savior should be shouted from the rooftops by believers the world over. But all too often, it is not. For a variety of reasons, many Christians keep their beliefs to themselves, and when they do, the world suffers because of their failure to speak up.

Paul shared a message to believers of every generation when he wrote, "God has not given us a spirit of timidity" (2 Timothy 1:7 NASB). Paul's meaning is clear: When sharing our testimonies, we must be courageous, forthright, and unashamed. As believers in Christ, we know how He has touched our hearts and changed our lives. Now is the time to share our personal testimonies with others.

The old familiar hymn begins, "What a friend we have in Jesus . . . ." No truer words were ever penned. Jesus is the sovereign Friend and ultimate Savior of mankind. Christ showed enduring love for His believers by willingly sacrificing His own life so that we might have eternal life. Let us love Him, praise Him, and share His message of salvation with our neighbors and with the world.

There is a glorified Man on the right hand of the Majesty in heaven faithfully representing us there. We are left for a season among men; let us faithfully represent Him here.

A. W. Tozer

Our faith grows by expression. If we want to keep our faith, we must share it. We must act.

Billy Graham

Jesus made Himself known to His own, and if others are to hear about Him today, you and I must tell them.

Vance Havner

For God has not given us a spirit of timidity, but of power and love and discipline. Therefore do not be ashamed of the testimony of our Lord . . . .

2 Timothy 1:7-8 NASB

Dear Lord, my life and my words bear testimony to my faith. Make me a faithful servant of Your Son, and let my testimony be worthy of You. Let me share Your Good News, Lord, and let my actions point others to You.

—

Amen

My Prayer for Today

Day 16

A Prayer for . . .

A GENEROUS HEART

Whenever we have the opportunity,
we should do good to everyone,
especially to our Christian brothers and sisters.

Galatians 6:10 NLT

The words of our Savior are clear: "Freely you have received, freely give" (Matthew 10:8 NIV). As followers of Christ, we are commanded to be generous with our friends, with our families, and with those in need. We must give freely of our time, our possessions, and, most especially, our love.

In 2 Corinthians 9, Paul reminds us that when we sow the seeds of generosity, we reap bountiful rewards in accordance with God's plan for our lives. But Paul offers a word of caution: We are commanded to be cheerful givers—not to give "grudgingly or under compulsion" (v. 7).

Today, take God's words to heart and make this pledge: Be a cheerful, generous, courageous giver. The world needs your help, and you need the spiritual rewards that will be yours when you do.

The mind grows by taking in,
but the heart grows by giving out.

Warren Wiersbe

Since you cannot do good to all, you are to pay special regard to those who, by the accidents of time or place or circumstances, are brought into closer connection with you.

St. Augustine

He climbs highest who helps another up.

Zig Ziglar

So let each one give as he purposes in his heart,
not grudgingly or of necessity;
for God loves a cheerful giver.

2 Corinthians 9:7 NKJV

A Prayer for Today

Lord, You have been so generous with me; let me be generous with others. Help me to give generously of my time and my possessions as I care for those in need. And, make me a humble giver, Lord, so that all the glory and the praise might be Yours.

—

Amen

My Prayer for Today

Day 17

A Prayer for . . .

THE COURAGE TO TRUST GOD

The LORD is my rock, and my fortress,
and my deliverer; my God, my strength,
in whom I will trust . . . .

Psalm 18:2 KJV

When our dreams come true and our plans prove successful, we find it easy to thank our Creator and easy to trust His divine providence. But in times of adversity and hardship, we may find ourselves questioning God's plans for our lives. In a letter to first-century Christians, Peter wrote, "And God, in his mighty power, will protect you until you receive this salvation, because you are trusting him" (1 Peter 1:5 NLT). These words remind us that when we trust God completely, He uses His mighty powers to protect us. The challenge for most of us is this: God expects us to trust Him in good times *and* bad.

On occasion, you will confront circumstances that trouble you to the very core of your soul. When you are afraid, trust in God. When you are worried, turn your concerns over to Him. When you are anxious, be still and listen for the quiet assurance of God's promises.

Do you aspire to do great things for God's kingdom? Then trust Him with every aspect of your life. Follow His commandments and pray for His guidance. Then, wait patiently for God's revelations and for His blessings. In His own fashion and in His own time, God will bless you in ways that you never could have imagined.

Troubles we bear trustfully can bring us
a fresh vision of God and a new outlook on life,
an outlook of peace and hope.

Billy Graham

We must trust God. We must trust not only
that he does what is best, but also
that he knows what is ahead.

Max Lucado

The more you give your mental burdens to
the Lord, the more exciting it becomes to see
how God will handle things that are impossible
for you to do anything about.

Charles Swindoll

In God, whose word I praise, in God I trust;
I will not be afraid.

Psalm 56:4 NIV

A Prayer for Today

Today, Lord, I will trust You and seek Your will for my life. You have a plan for me, Father. Let me discover it and live it, knowing that when I trust in You, I am eternally blessed.

—

Amen

My Prayer for Today

Day 18

A Prayer for . . .

A HUMBLE HEART

For everyone who exalts himself will be humbled, and the one who humbles himself will be exalted.

Luke 14:11 HCSB

When we experience success, it's easy to puff out our chests and proclaim, "I did that!" But it's wrong. Dietrich Bonhoeffer was correct when he observed, "It is very easy to overestimate the importance of our own achievements in comparison with what we owe others." In other words, reality breeds humility.

Who are the greatest among us? Are they the proud and the powerful? Hardly. The greatest among us are the humble servants who care less for their own glory and more for God's glory. If we seek greatness in God's eyes, we must forever praise God's good works, not our own.

If you're tempted to overestimate your own accomplishments, resist that temptation. Instead of puffing out your chest and saying, "Look at me!", give credit where credit is due, starting with God. And, rest assured: There is no such thing as a self-made man. All of us are made by God . . . and He deserves the glory, not us.

A humble heart is like a magnet that draws the favor of God toward us.

Jim Cymbala

Humility is the exhibition of the spirit of Jesus Christ and is the touchstone of saintliness.

Oswald Chambers

It was pride that changed angels into devils; it is humility that makes men as angels.

St. Augustine

It is better to live humbly with the poor than to share plunder with the proud.

Proverbs 16:19 NLT

Heavenly Father, it is the nature of mankind to be prideful, and I am no exception. When I am boastful, keep me mindful that all my gifts come from You. When I feel prideful, remind me that You sent Your Son to be a humble carpenter. Let me grow beyond my need for earthly praise, God, and let me look only to You for approval. You are the Giver of all things good; let me give all the glory to You.

—

Amen

MY PRAYER FOR TODAY

Day 19

A Prayer for . . .

DELIVERANCE FROM TEMPTATION

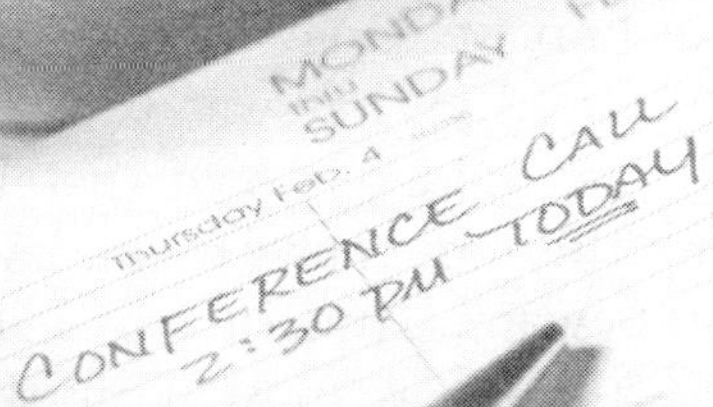

My son, if sinners entice you, do not consent.

Proverbs 1:10 NKJV

Because our world is filled with temptations, we confront them at every turn. Some of these temptations are small—eating a second piece of chocolate cake, for example. Too much cake may cause us to defile, at least in a modest way, the bodily temple that God has entrusted to our care. This will not bring us to our knees. Other temptations, however, are not so harmless.

The devil, it seems, is working overtime these days, and causing pain and heartache in more places and in more ways than ever before. We, as Christians, must remain vigilant. Not only must we resist Satan when he confronts us, but we must also avoid those places where Satan can most easily tempt us. And, if we are to avoid the unending temptations of this world, we must arm ourselves with the Word of God.

In a letter to believers, Peter offered a stern warning: "Your adversary, the devil, prowls around like a roaring lion, seeking someone to devour" (1 Peter 5:8 NASB). What was true in Peter's time is equally true in our own. Satan tempts his prey and then devours them. As Christians, we must beware. And, if we seek righteousness in our own lives, we must earnestly wrap ourselves in the protection of God's Holy Word. When we do, we are secure.

It is not the Word hidden in the head
that keeps us from sin.
It is the Word hidden in the heart.

Vance Havner

Since you are tempted without ceasing,
pray without ceasing.

C. H. Spurgeon

Because Christ has faced our every temptation without sin, we never face a temptation that has no door of escape.

Beth Moore

No temptation has overtaken you but such as is common to man; and God is faithful, who will not allow you to be tempted beyond what you are able, but with the temptation will provide the way of escape.

1 Corinthians 10:13 NASB

A Prayer for Today

Dear Lord, this world is filled with temptations, distractions, and frustrations. When I turn my thoughts away from You and Your Word, Lord, I suffer bitter consequences. But, when I trust in Your commandments, I am safe. Direct my path far from the temptations and distractions of the world. Let me discover Your will and follow it, Dear Lord, this day and always.

—

Amen

My Prayer for Today

Day 20

A Prayer for . . .

STRENGTH IN ADVERSITY

For though a righteous man falls seven times,
he rises again . . . .

Proverbs 24:16 NIV

From time to time, all of us face adversity, hardship, disappointment, and loss. Old Man Trouble pays periodic visits to each of us; none of us are exempt. When we are troubled, God stands ready and willing to protect us. Our responsibility, of course, is to ask Him for protection. When we call upon Him in heartfelt prayer, He will answer—in His own time and in accordance with His own perfect plan.

Our world continues to change, but God's love remains constant. And, He remains ready to comfort us and strengthen us whenever we turn to Him. Psalm 145 promises, "The LORD is near to all who call on him, to all who call on him in truth. He fulfills the desires of those who fear him; he hears their cry and saves them" (vv. 18-20 NIV).

Life is often challenging, but as Christians, we must not be afraid. God loves us, and He will protect us. In times of hardship, He will comfort us; in times of sorrow, He will dry our tears. When we are troubled or weak or sorrowful, God is always with us. We must build our lives on the rock that cannot be shaken . . . we must trust in God. Always.

There are four essentials for victory in trials: a joyful attitude, an understanding mind, a surrendered will, and a heart that wants to believe.

Warren Wiersbe

It may be the most difficult time of your life. You may be enduring your own whirlwind. But the whirlwind is a temporary experience. Your faithful, caring Lord will see you through.

Charles Swindoll

Trouble is one of God's great servants because it reminds us how much we continually need the Lord.

Jim Cymbala

When my heart is overwhelmed: lead me to the rock that is higher than I.

Psalm 61:2 KJV

Heavenly Father, You are my strength and my refuge. As I journey through this day, I know that I may encounter disappointments and losses. When I am troubled, let me turn to You. Keep me steady, Lord, and renew a right spirit inside of me this day and forever.

—

Amen

MY PRAYER FOR TODAY

Day 21

A Prayer for . . .

THE WISDOM TO BE A WORTHY EXAMPLE

Be an example to the believers in word,
in conduct, in love, in spirit, in faith, in purity.

1 Timothy 4:12 NKJV

Whether we like it or not, all of us are examples. The question is not *whether* we will be examples to our families and friends; the question is simply *what kind* of examples will we be.

What kind of example are you? Are you the kind of man whose life serves as a powerful example of righteousness? Are you a man whose behavior serves as a positive role model for young people? Are you the kind of man whose actions, day in and day out, are based upon integrity, fidelity, and a love for the Lord? If so, you are not only blessed by God, but you are also a powerful force for good in a world that desperately needs positive influences such as yours.

D. L. Moody advised, "A man ought to live so that everybody knows he is a Christian, and most of all, his family ought to know." And that's sound advice because our families and friends are watching . . . and so, for that matter, is God.

A holy life will produce the deepest impression.
Lighthouses blow no horns; they only shine.

D. L. Moody

In our faith we follow in someone's steps.
In our faith we leave footprints to guide others.
It's the principle of discipleship.

Max Lucado

Be to the world a sign that while we as
Christians do not have all the answers,
we do know and care about the questions.

Billy Graham

In everything set them an example
by doing what is good.

Titus 2:7 NIV

Lord, make me a worthy example to my family and friends. And, let my words and my deeds serve as a testimony to the changes You have made in my life. Let me praise You, Father, by following in the footsteps of Your Son, and let others see Him through me.

—

Amen

MY PRAYER FOR TODAY

My Hopes & Prayers for Next Week

My Hopes & Prayers for Next Week

Day 22

A Prayer for . . .

INTEGRITY

The man of integrity walks securely,
but he who takes crooked paths
will be found out.

Proverbs 10:9 NIV

Honesty is the best policy, but it is not always the *easiest* policy. Sometimes, the truth hurts, and sometimes it's tough to be a man of integrity . . . tough, but essential.

Charles Swindoll correctly observed, "Nothing speaks louder or more powerfully than a life of integrity." Godly men agree.

Integrity is built slowly over a lifetime. It is the sum of every right decision and every honest word. It is forged on the anvil of honorable work and polished by the twin virtues of honesty and fairness. Integrity is a precious thing—difficult to build but easy to tear down. As believers in Christ, we must seek to live each day with discipline, honesty, and faith. When we do, integrity becomes a habit. And God smiles.

Integrity is not a given factor in everyone's life.
It is a result of self-discipline, inner trust,
and a decision to be relentlessly honest
in all situations in our lives.

John Maxwell

In matters of style, swim with the current.
In matters of principle, stand like a rock.

Thomas Jefferson

Integrity is the glue that holds our way of life together. We must constantly strive to keep our integrity intact. When wealth is lost, nothing is lost; when health is lost, something is lost; when character is lost, all is lost.

Billy Graham

Till I die, I will not deny my integrity.
I will maintain my righteousness and
never let go of it; my conscience will not
reproach me as long as I live.

Job 27:5-6 NIV

A Prayer for Today

Dear Lord, You command Your children to walk in truth. Let me follow Your commandment. Give me the courage to speak honestly, and let me walk righteously with You so that others might see Your eternal truth reflected in my words and my deeds.

—

Amen

My Prayer for Today

Day 23

A Prayer for . . .

PATIENCE

A man's wisdom gives him patience;
it is to his glory to overlook an offense.

Proverbs 19:11 NIV

We human beings are, by our very nature, impatient. We are impatient with others, impatient with ourselves, and impatient with our Creator. We want things to happen according to our own timetables, but our Heavenly Father may have other plans. That's why we must learn the art of patience.

Psalm 37:7 commands us to "rest in the LORD, and wait patiently for Him" (NKJV). But, for most of us, waiting patiently for Him is difficult. Why? Because we are fallible human beings who seek solutions to our problems today, if not sooner. Still, God instructs us to wait patiently for His plans to unfold, and that's exactly what we should do.

So the next time you find yourself drumming your fingers as you wait for a quick resolution to the challenges of everyday living, take a deep breath and ask God for patience. Be still before your Heavenly Father and trust His timetable: it's the peaceful way to live.

God freely admits he is holding back his power, but he restrains himself for our benefit. For all scoffers who call for direct action from the heavens, the prophets have ominous advice: Just wait.

Philip Yancey

God is in no hurry. Compared to the works of mankind, He is extremely deliberate. God is not a slave to the human clock.

Charles Swindoll

If only we could be as patient with other people as God is with us!

Jim Gallery

Patience is better than pride.

Ecclesiastes 7:8 NLT

A Prayer for Today

Heavenly Father, let me wait quietly for You. Let me live according to Your plan and according to Your timetable. When I am hurried, slow me down. When I become impatient with others, give me empathy. Today, I want to be a patient Christian, Dear Lord, as I trust in You and in Your master plan.

—

Amen

My Prayer for Today

Day 24
A Prayer for . . .

GOD'S BLESSINGS

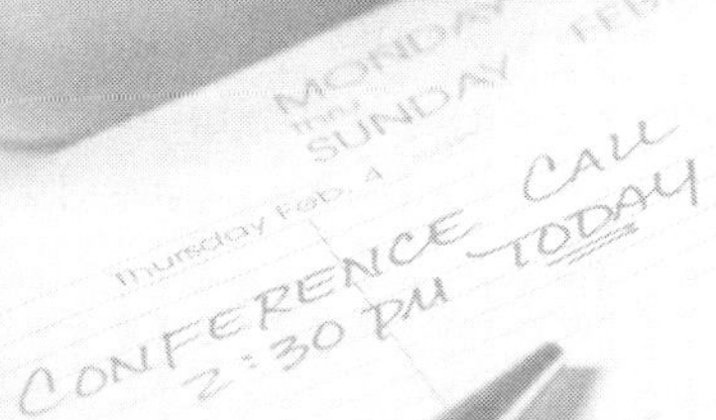

Blessings crown the head of the righteous . . . .

Proverbs 10:6 NIV

Have you counted your blessings lately? You should. Of course, God's gifts are too numerous to count, but as a grateful Christian, you should attempt to count them nonetheless.

Your blessings include life, family, friends, talents, and possessions, for starters. And your greatest gift—a treasure that was paid for on the cross and is yours for the asking—is God's gift of salvation through Christ Jesus.

As believing Christians, we have all been blessed beyond measure. Thus, thanksgiving should become a habit, a regular part of our daily routines. Today, let us pause and thank our Creator for His blessings. And let us demonstrate our gratitude to the Giver of all things good by using His gifts and by sharing them.

God blesses us in spite of our lives
and not because of our lives.

Max Lucado

Think of the blessings we so easily take for granted: Life itself; preservation from danger; every bit of health we enjoy; every hour of liberty; the ability to see, to hear, to speak, to think, and to imagine all this comes from the hand of God.

Billy Graham

We do not need to beg Him to bless us;
He simply cannot help it.

Hannah Whitall Smith

I will bless them and the places surrounding my hill. I will send down showers in season; there will be showers of blessings.

Ezekiel 34:26 NIV

Lord, I have more blessings than I can possibly count; make me mindful of Your precious gifts. You have cared for me, Lord, and You have saved me. I will give thanks and praise You always. Today, let me share Your blessings with others, just as You first shared them with me.

—

Amen

My Prayer for Today

Day 25

A Prayer for . . .

OPTIMISM AND HOPE

For God has not given us a spirit of fear,
but of power and of love and of a sound mind.

2 Timothy 1:7 NLT

Are you an optimistic, hopeful, enthusiastic Christian? You should be. After all, as a believer, you have every reason to be optimistic about life here on earth *and* life eternal. As C. H. Spurgeon observed, "Our hope in Christ for the future is the mainstream of our joy." But sometimes, you may find yourself pulled down by the inevitable demands and worries of life here on earth. If you find yourself discouraged, exhausted, or both, then it's time to take your concerns to God. When you do, He will lift your sprits and renew your strength.

Today, make this promise to yourself and keep it: vow to be a hope-filled Christian. Think optimistically about your life, your profession, your family, and your future. Trust your hopes, not your fears. Take time to celebrate God's glorious creation. And then, when you've filled your heart with hope and gladness, share your optimism with others. They'll be better for it, and so will you.

Hope must be in the future tense.
Faith, to be faith, must always be
in the present tense.

Catherine Marshall

Keep your feet on the ground, but let your heart soar as high as it will. Refuse to be average or to surrender to the chill of your spiritual environment.

A. W. Tozer

If our hearts have been attuned to God through an abiding faith in Christ, the result will be joyous optimism and good cheer.

Billy Graham

For God has not given us a spirit of fearfulness, but one of power, love, and sound judgment.

2 Timothy 1:7 HCSB

Lord, let me be an expectant Christian. Let me expect the best from You, and let me look for the best in others. If I become discouraged, Father, turn my thoughts and my prayers to You. Let me trust You, Lord, to direct my life. And, let me be Your faithful, hopeful, optimistic servant every day that I live.

—

Amen

My Prayer for Today

Day 26

A Prayer for . . .

SPIRITUAL GROWTH

But grow in the grace and knowledge of our Lord and Savior Jesus Christ.

2 Peter 3:18 NIV

Plants of every sort respond to nourishment, and so it is with human hearts. When we begin each day with heads bowed and hearts lifted, we remind ourselves of God's love, His protection, and His commandments. If we are wise, we align our priorities for the coming day with the teachings and commandments that God has given us through His Holy Word. And because we nourish our souls, we continue to grow "in the grace and knowledge of our Lord."

The journey toward spiritual maturity lasts a lifetime. As Christians, we can and should continue to grow in our devotion to the Savior as long as we live. When we cease to grow, either emotionally or spiritually, we do ourselves a profound disservice. But, if we study God's Word, if we obey His commandments, and if we live in the center of His will, we will not be "stagnant" believers. We will, instead, be growing Christians, and that's exactly what God intends for us to become.

You are free to choose, but the choices you make today will determine what you will have, what you will be, and what you will do in the tomorrow of your life.

Zig Ziglar

Grass that is here today and gone tomorrow does not require much time to mature. A big oak tree that lasts for generations requires much more time to grow and mature. God is concerned about your life through eternity. Allow Him to take all the time He needs to shape you for His purposes. Larger assignments will require longer periods of preparation.

Henry Blackaby

Know the love of Christ which surpasses knowledge, that you may be filled up to all the fullness of God.

Ephesians 3:19 NASB

A Prayer for Today

Dear Lord, when I open myself to You, I am blessed. Let me accept Your love and Your wisdom, Father. Show me Your way, and deliver me from the painful mistakes that I make when I stray from Your commandments. Let me live according to Your Word, and let me grow in my faith every day that I live.

—

Amen

My Prayer for Today

Day 27

A Prayer for . . .

WILLING HANDS

He who works his land will have abundant food, but the one who chases fantasies will have his fill of poverty.

Proverbs 28:19 NIV

God's Word teaches us the value of hard work. In his second letter to the Thessalonians, Paul warns, " . . . if any would not work, neither should he eat" (3:10 KJV). And the Book of Proverbs proclaims, "One who is slack in his work is brother to one who destroys" (18:9 NIV). In short, God has created a world in which diligence is rewarded but sloth is not. So, whatever it is that you choose to do, do it with commitment, excitement, and vigor.

Hard work is not simply a proven way to get ahead; it's also part of God's plan for you. God did not create you for a life of mediocrity; He created you for far greater things. Reaching for greater things usually requires work and lots of it, which is perfectly fine with God. After all, He knows that you're up to the task, and He has big plans for you *if* you possess a loving heart *and* willing hands.

We are expected to use all available means. We are not allowed to be idle and do nothing simply because we say we are trusting in providence.

C. H. Spurgeon

Ordinary work, which is what most of us do most of the time, is ordained by God every bit as much as is the extraordinary.

Elisabeth Elliot

It may be that the day of judgment will dawn tomorrow; in that case, we shall gladly stop working for a better tomorrow. But not before.

Dietrich Bonhoeffer

Work hard, but not just to please your masters when they are watching. As slaves of Christ, do the will of God with all your heart. Work with enthusiasm, as though you were working for the Lord rather than for people.

Ephesians 6:6-7 NLT

Lord, I know that You desire a bountiful harvest for all Your children. But, You have instructed us that we must sow before we reap, not after. Help me, Lord, to sow the seeds of Your abundance everywhere I go. Let me be diligent in all my undertakings and give me patience to wait for Your harvest. In time, Lord, let me reap the harvest that is found in Your will for my life.

—

Amen

My Prayer for Today

Day 28

A Prayer for . . .

FAITHFUL STEWARDSHIP

As each one has received a gift,
minister it to one another, as good stewards of
the manifold grace of God.

1 Peter 4:10 NKJV

As believers, we are challenged to be faithful stewards of the gifts and talents that God has given us. But we live in a world that encourages us to do otherwise. Ours is a society that is filled to the brim with countless opportunities to squander our time and our talents. But we must beware: God instructs us never to squander the gifts that He bestows upon us.

All of us have special gifts, and you are no exception. Today, accept this challenge: value the talent that God has given you, nourish it, make it grow, and share it with the world. After all, the best way to say "Thank You" for God's gifts is to use them.

God has given gifts to each of you from his great variety of spiritual gifts. Manage them well so that God's generosity can flow through you.

1 Peter 4:10 NLT

A steward does not own, but instead manages, all that his master puts into his hands.

Warren Wiersbe

Let a man so consider us, as servants of Christ and stewards of the mysteries of God. Moreover it is required in stewards that one be found faithful.

1 Corinthians 4:1-2 NKJV

Dear Lord, make me a faithful steward of my possessions, my talents, my time, and my testimony. In every aspect of my life, Father, let me be Your humble, obedient servant. I trust, Father, that You will provide for me now and throughout eternity. And I will obey Your commandment that I give sacrificially to the needs of Your Church.

—

Amen

MY PRAYER FOR TODAY

My Hopes & Prayers for Next Week

My Hopes & Prayers for Next Week

Day 29

A Prayer for . . .

WISDOM

Trust in the LORD with all thine heart;
and lean not unto thine own understanding.
In all thy ways acknowledge him,
and he shall direct thy paths.

Proverbs 3:5-6 KJV

Do you seek to be the righteous man that your Heavenly Father intends you to be? Then you must seek God's wisdom and obey His commandments. But even if you study God's Word carefully, don't expect to become instantly wise.

Wisdom is not like a mushroom; it does not spring up overnight. It is, instead, like an oak tree that starts as a tiny acorn, grows into a sapling, and eventually reaches up to the sky, tall and strong.

To become wise, you should seek out worthy mentors and listen carefully to their advice. To become wise, you must associate, day in and day out, with godly men and women. And, you must act in accordance with God's laws. When you do, your wisdom will grow day by day, and you will be a blessing to your family, to your friends, and to the world.

Let your old age be childlike, and childhood like old age; that is, so that neither may your wisdom be with pride, nor your humility without wisdom.

St. Augustine

Knowledge can be found in books or in school. Wisdom, on the other hand, starts with God . . . and ends there.

Marie T. Freeman

The doorstep to the temple of wisdom is a knowledge of our own ignorance.

C. H. Spurgeon

But the wisdom that is from above is first pure, then peaceable, gentle, willing to yield, full of mercy and good fruits, without partiality and without hypocrisy.

James 3:17 NKJV

A Prayer for Today

Lord, make me a man of wisdom and discernment. I seek wisdom, Lord, not from this world but from You. Lead me in Your ways and teach me from Your Word so that, in time, my wisdom might glorify Your kingdom and Your Son.

—

Amen

My Prayer for Today

Day 30

A Prayer for . . .

THE COURAGE TO LEAD

Those who are wise will shine like
the brightness of the heavens, and those who
lead many to righteousness, like the stars
for ever and ever.

Daniel 12:3 NIV

Our world needs Christian leaders who willingly honor God with their words and their deeds, but not necessarily in that order.

If you seek to be a godly leader, then you must begin by being a worthy example to your family, to your friends, to your church, and to your community. After all, your words of instruction will never ring true unless you yourself are willing to follow them.

Are you the kind of leader whom you would want to follow? If so, congratulations. But if the answer to that question is no, then it's time to improve your leadership skills, beginning with the words that you speak *and* the example that you set, but not necessarily in that order.

You can never separate a leader's actions from his character.

John Maxwell

Leaders must learn how to wait. Often their followers don't always see as far as they see or have the faith that they have.

Warren Wiersbe

Be an example to the believers in word, in conduct, in love, in spirit, in faith, in purity.

1 Timothy 4:12 NKJV

His lord said unto him, Well done, thou good and faithful servant: thou hast been faithful over a few things, I will make thee ruler over many things: enter thou into the joy of thy lord.

Matthew 25:21 KJV

A Prayer for Today

Heavenly Father, when I find myself in a position of leadership, let me follow Your teachings and obey Your commandments. Make me a person of integrity and wisdom, Lord, and make me a worthy example to those whom I serve. And, let me turn to You, Lord, for guidance and for strength in all that I say and do.

—

Amen

My Prayer for Today

Day 31

A Prayer for . . .

SALVATION

For God so loved the world that he gave
his one and only Son, that whoever believes in
him shall not perish but have eternal life.

John 3:16 NIV

How marvelous it is that God became a man and walked among us. Had He not chosen to do so, we might feel removed from a distant Creator. But ours is not a distant God. Ours is a God who understands—far better than we ever could—the essence of what it means to be human.

God understands our hopes, our fears, and our temptations. He understands what it means to be angry and what it costs to forgive. He knows the heart, the conscience, and the soul of every person who has ever lived, including you. And God has a plan of salvation that is intended for you. Accept it. Accept God's gift through the person of His Son Christ Jesus, and then rest assured: God walked among us so that you might have eternal life; amazing though it may seem, He did it for you.

God is not saving the world; it is done.
Our business is to get men
and women to realize it.
Oswald Chambers

Salvation is God's sudden, calming presence
during the stormy seas of our lives.
Max Lucado

We are not saved by believing the Bible,
but by trusting the Christ
who is revealed in the Bible.
Warren Wiersbe

He alone is my rock and my salvation;
he is my fortress, I will never be shaken.
Psalm 62:2 NIV

A Prayer for Today

Lord, I am only here on this earth for a brief while. But, You have offered me the priceless gift of eternal life through Your Son Jesus. I accept Your gift, Lord, with thanksgiving and praise. And today, help me share the Good News of my salvation with all those who need Your healing touch.

—

Amen

My Prayer for Today

My Hopes & Prayers for Next Month

My Hopes & Prayers for Next Month

MY HOPES & PRAYERS FOR NEXT MONTH

My Hopes & Prayers for Next Month

SELECTED SCRIPTURE

ANGER

All bitterness, anger and wrath, insult and slander must be removed from you, along with all wickedness. And be kind and compassionate to one another, forgiving one another, just as God also forgave you in Christ.

Ephesians 4:31-32 HCSB

Better a patient man than a warrior, a man who controls his temper than one who takes a city.

Proverbs 16:32 NIV

Stop your anger! Turn from your rage! Do not envy others—it only leads to harm.

Psalm 37:8 NLT

For God hath not appointed us to wrath, but to obtain salvation by our Lord Jesus Christ . . . .

1 Thessalonians 5:9 KJV

If anyone considers himself
religious and yet does not keep
a tight rein on his tongue,
he deceives himself and
his religion is worthless.

James 1:26 NIV

WORRY

Let not your heart be troubled;
you believe in God, believe also in Me.

John 14:1 NKJV

So do not worry, saying, "What shall we eat?" or "What shall we drink?" or "What shall we wear?" For the pagans run after all these things, and your heavenly Father knows that you need them. But seek first his kingdom and his righteousness, and all these things will be given to you as well. Therefore do not worry about tomorrow, for tomorrow will worry about itself. Each day has enough trouble of its own.

Matthew 6:31-34 NIV

For this reason I say to you, do not be worried about your life, as to what you will eat or what you will drink; nor for your body, as to what you will put on. Is not life more than food, and the body more than clothing? Look at the birds of the air, that they do not sow, nor reap nor gather into barns, and yet your heavenly Father feeds them. Are you not worth much more than they?

Matthew 6:25-26 NASB

Don't worry about anything; instead, pray about everything. Tell God what you need, and thank him for all he has done.

Philippians 4:6 NLT

BEHAVIOR

Even a child is known by his actions,
by whether his conduct is pure and right.

Proverbs 20:11 NIV

Therefore, get your minds ready for action, being self-disciplined, and set your hope completely on the grace to be brought to you at the revelation of Jesus Christ. As obedient children, do not be conformed to the desires of your former ignorance but, as the One who called you is holy, you also are to be holy in all your conduct.

1 Peter 1:13-15 HCSB

A good person produces good deeds from a good heart, and an evil person produces evil deeds from an evil heart. Whatever is in your heart determines what you say.

Luke 6:45 NLT

Abhor that which is evil;
cleave to that which is good.

Romans 12:9 KJV

LOVE

Love is patient, love is kind and is not jealous; love does not brag and is not arrogant, does not act unbecomingly; it does not seek its own, is not provoked, does not take into account a wrong suffered, does not rejoice in unrighteousness, but rejoices with the truth; bears all things, believes all things, hopes all things, endures all things.

1 Corinthians 13:4–7 NASB

He who does not love does not know God, for God is love.

1 John 4:8 NKJV

And the most important piece of clothing you must wear is love. Love is what binds us all together in perfect harmony.

Colossians 3:14 NLT

Beloved, if God so loved us, we ought also to love one another.

1 John 4:11 KJV

And now abide faith, hope,
love, these three;
but the greatest of these is love.

1 Corinthians 13:13 NKJV

MIRACLES

You are the God who performs miracles;
you display your power among the peoples.

Psalm 77:14 NIV

God verified the message by signs and wonders and various miracles and by giving gifts of the Holy Spirit whenever he chose to do so.

Hebrews 2:4 NLT

Jesus said to them, "I have shown you many great miracles from the Father."

John 10:32 NIV

That is what the Scriptures mean when they say, "No eye has seen, no ear has heard, and no mind has imagined what God has prepared for those who love him."

1 Corinthians 2:9 NLT

For with God
nothing shall be impossible.

Luke 1:37 KJV